Oxford Reading Tree

Level 1+

Floppy's Phonics

Activity Book

1

Debbie Hepplewhite

OXFORD

Say the sounds

s	a	t	p

i	n	m	d

g	o	c	k

-ck	e	u	r

h	b	f	-ff

l	-ll	-le	-ss

Practise the sound

Say the sound. Trace the letter.

Say the word. Listen for the /s/ sound.

Point and say the sound.

Say the sound. Trace the letters. Write the letters.

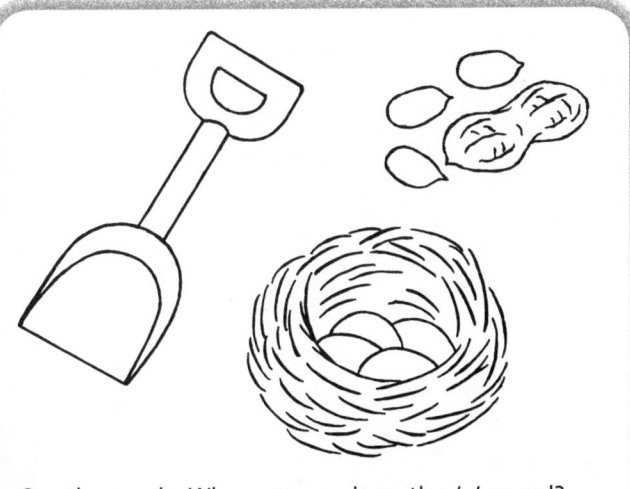

Say the words. When can you hear the /s/ sound?

Draw something beginning with **s**.

s

2

Practise the sound

Say the sound. Trace the letter.

Say the word. Listen for the /a/ sound.

a 🍎 a 🍎 a a 🍎 a a

🍎 a 🍎 a 🍎 a a 🍎 a a a

Point and say the sound.

Say the sound. Trace the letters. Write the letters.

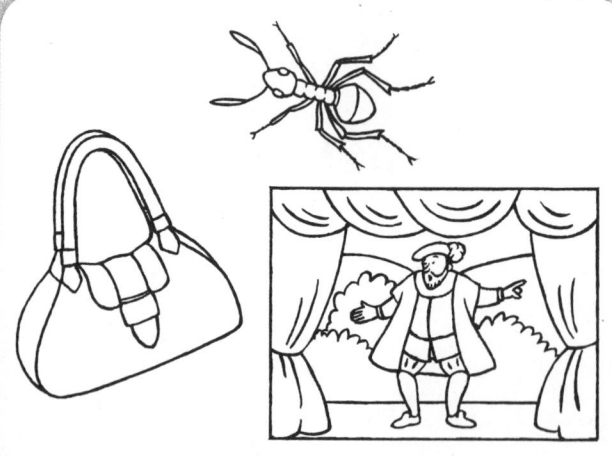

Say the words. When can you hear the /a/ sound?

Draw something beginning with **a**.

s **a**

Practise the sound

Say the sound. Trace the letter.

Say the word. Listen for the /t/ sound.

t a t t s t a t s

at sat at sat at sat

Point and say the sounds. Sound out and blend to read the words.

 t t t t

Say the sound. Trace the letters. Write the letters.

Say the words. When can you hear the /t/ sound?

Draw something beginning with **t**.

 s a t

Practise the sound

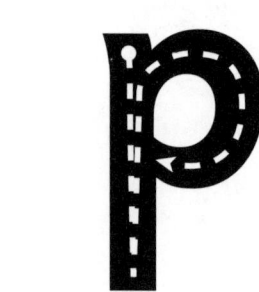

Say the sound. Trace the letter.

Say the word. Listen for the /p/ sound.

p t s a t p s a p

pat tap pat taps pats

Point and say the sounds. Sound out and blend to read the words.

 p p p

Say the sound. Trace the letters. Write the letters.

Say the words. When can you hear the /p/ sound?

Draw something beginning with **p**.

 s a t **p**

Practise the sound

Say the sound. Trace the letter.

Say the word. Listen for the /i/ sound.

i   s   p   i   a   t   i   s   p   t

it   sit   is   tip   sit   it   is

its   pit   pip   sip   its   pips

Point and say the sounds. Sound out and blend to read the words.

Say the sound. Trace the letters. Write the letters.

Say the words. When can you hear the /i/ sound?

Draw something beginning with **i**.

s   a   t   p   **i**

6

Practise the sound

Say the sound. Trace the letter.

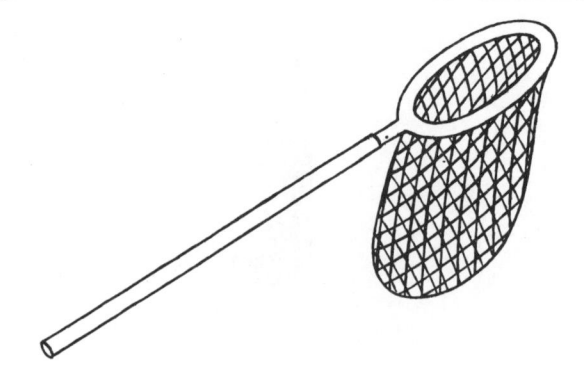

Say the word. Listen for the /n/ sound.

n s i a p t n s i

an nip in tin tan ant

nap pin pan ants pins

Point and say the sounds. Sound out and blend to read the words.

n n n n

Say the sound. Trace the letters. Write the letters.

Say the words. When can you hear the /n/ sound?

Draw something beginning with **n**.

s a t p i **n**

Practise the sound

Say the sound. Trace the letter.

Say the word. Listen for the /m/ sound.

m a t m p n i s p

map mat am amp Pam

man Tim maps mint

Point and say the sounds. Sound out and blend to read the words.

m m m m m

Say the sound. Trace the letters. Write the letters.

Say the words. When can you hear the /m/ sound?

Draw something beginning with **m**.

s a t p i n **m**

Practise the sound

Say the sound. Trace the letter.

Say the word. Listen for the /d/ sound.

d m n p a d t s d

dip pad sad dad and

dips sand damp

Point and say the sounds. Sound out and blend to read the words.

d d d d

Say the sound. Trace the letters. Write the letters.

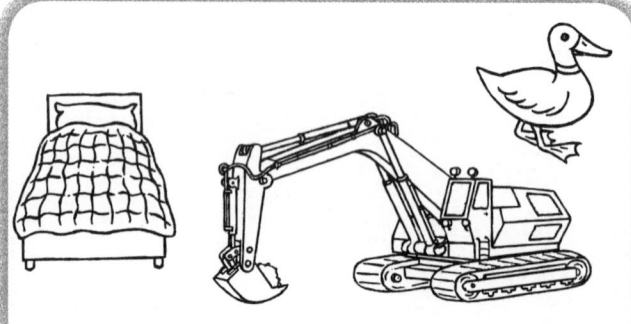

Say the words. When can you hear the /d/ sound?

Draw something beginning with **d**.

s a t p i n m **d**

Practise the sound

Say the sound. Trace the letter.

Say the word. Listen for the /g/ sound.

g s m p a g d g t

dig gas tag gap digs

nag sag gaps stag

Point and say the sounds. Sound out and blend to read the words.

 g g g g

Say the sound. Trace the letters. Write the letters.

Say the words. When can you hear the /g/ sound?

Draw something beginning with **g**.

s a t p i n m d **g**

Practise the sound

Say the sound. Trace the letter.

Say the word. Listen for the /o/ sound.

o m d g s a o n o

pot dog got dot on

nod dots spot pond

Point and say the sounds. Sound out and blend to read the words.

   o

Say the sound. Trace the letters. Write the letters.

Say the words. When can you hear the /o/ sound?

Draw something beginning with o.

s a t p i n m d g **o**

Practise the sound

Say the sound. Trace the letter.

Say the word. Listen for the /k/ sound.

c g m p c i t n c

cap cot can cat act

cats camp cost picnic

Point and say the sounds. Sound out and blend to read the words.

c c c c c

Say the sound. Trace the letters. Write the letters.

Say the words. When can you hear the /k/ sound?

Draw something beginning with **c**.

a t p i n m d g o c

Practise the sound

Say the sound. Trace the letter.

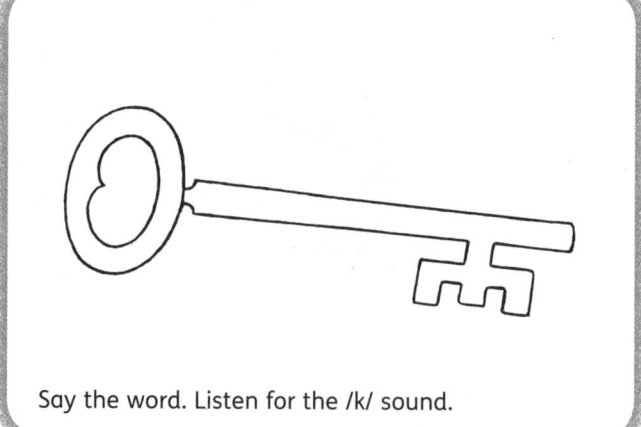

Say the word. Listen for the /k/ sound.

k i m g d k n t k

kit   kip   kid   kits   kin

skip   kids   skin   skim

Sound out and blend to read the words.

 k k k k

Say the sound. Trace the letters. Write the letters.

Say the words. When can you hear the /k/ sound?

Draw something beginning with **k**.

 t p i n m d g o c **k**

Practise the sound

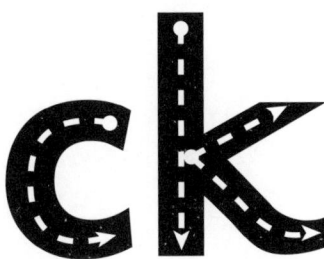

Say the sound. Trace the letters.

Say the word. Listen for the /k/ sound.

sack pick pack kick

tick-tock sock clock

snack stack sticks stock

Sound out and blend to read the words.

ck ck ck ck

Say the sound. Trace the letters. Write the letters.

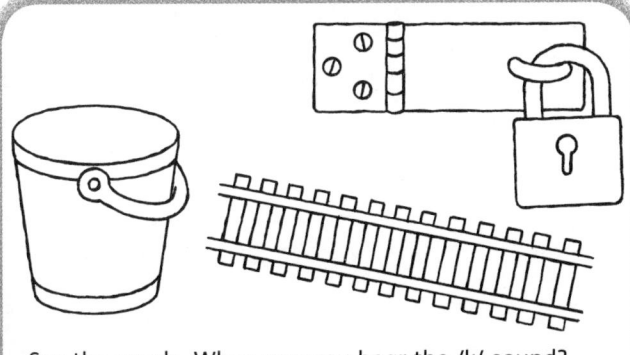

Say the words. When can you hear the /k/ sound?

Draw something ending in **ck**.

p i n m d g o c k -**ck**

14

Practise your reading and writing

Spell and write words with the focus grapheme.

1. A cat is in a sack.

2. Pick the socks to pack, Tom!

Blend to read the words and sentences.

Draw and label a picture to match one of the sentences.

Practise the sound

Say the sound. Trace the letter.

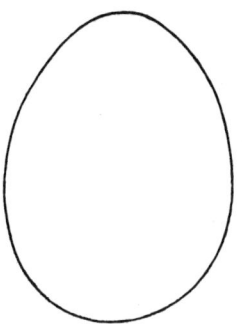

Say the word. Listen for the /e/ sound.

men net pen set den

peg get neck peck nets

deck pets sent mend

Sound out and blend to read the words.

 e e e

Say the sound. Trace the letters. Write the letters.

Say the words. When can you hear the /e/ sound?

Draw something beginning with **e**.

 i n m d g o c k -ck **e**

Practise your reading and writing

Spell and write words with the focus grapheme.

1. The pet can peck.

2. Ten men get a tent.

Blend to read the words and sentences.

Draw and label a picture to match one of the sentences.

Practise the sound

Say the sound. Trace the letter.

Say the word. Listen for the /u/ sound.

up   tug   cup   sun   cut

dug   mud   duck   tuck

must   dump   pump   stuck

Sound out and blend to read the words.

u   u   u   u

Say the sound. Trace the letters. Write the letters.

Say the words. When can you hear the /u/ sound?

Draw something beginning with **u**.

n   m   d   g   o   c   k   -ck   e   **u**

Practise your reading and writing

Spell and write words with the focus grapheme.

1. A dog is in the mud and muck.

2. The duck digs and pecks in the mud.

Blend to read the words and sentences.

Draw and label a picture to match one of the sentences.

Practise the sound

Say the sound. Trace the letter.

Say the word. Listen for the /r/ sound.

run rug red rip rod

rock rats drop rest

dress crack drumstick

Sound out and blend to read the words.

Say the sound. Trace the letters. Write the letters.

Say the words. When can you hear the /r/ sound?

Draw something beginning with **r**.

m d g o c k -ck e u r

Practise your reading and writing

Spell and write words with the focus grapheme.

1. A rat is on the red rug.

2. The red rocket rockets up the ramp.

Blend to read the words and sentences.

Draw and label a picture to match one of the sentences.

Practise the sound

Say the sound. Trace the letter.

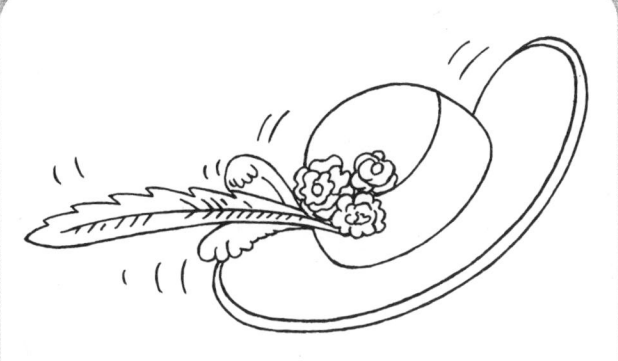

Say the word. Listen for the /h/ sound.

hot hen hat had hens

hops hip hop hit

hand hunt hum hi<u>dd</u>en

Sound out and blend to read the words.

h h h h

Say the sound. Trace the letters. Write the letters.

Say the words. When can you hear the /h/ sound?

Draw something beginning with **h**.

d g o c k -ck e u r h

Practise your reading and writing

Spell and write words with the focus grapheme.

1. A rat is in a hat.

2. The hen hops and pecks in the mud.

Blend to read the words and sentences.

Draw and label a picture to match one of the sentences.

Practise the sound

Say the sound. Trace the letter.

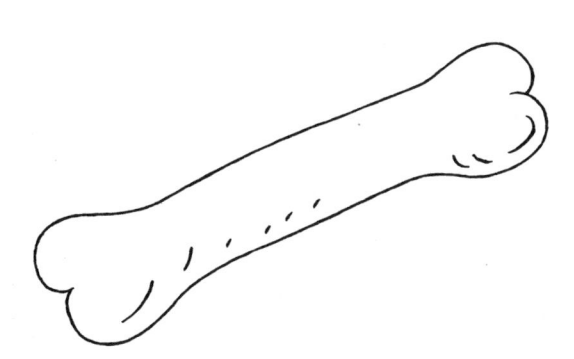

Say the word. Listen for the /b/ sound.

big bun bed bag back

bits bobs bats bend

bump crab bags rabbit

Sound out and blend to read the words.

b b b b

Say the sound. Trace the letters. Write the letters.

Say the words. When can you hear the /b/ sound?

Draw something beginning with **b**.

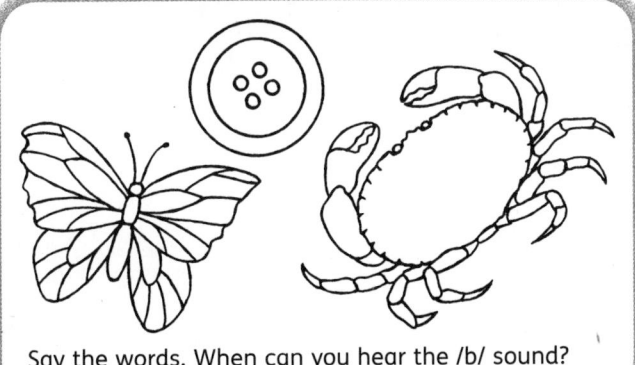

 g o c k -ck e u r h **b**

Practise your reading and writing

Spell and write words with the focus grapheme.

1. A big bug hops on a stick.

2. The big bug begs the duck and the hen not to peck it.

Blend to read the words and sentences.

Draw and label a picture to match one of the sentences.

Practise the sound

Say the sound. Trace the letter.

Say the word. Listen for the /f/ sound.

fin fun fog fed fat

if fan fist frog soft

figs facts drift of

Sound out and blend to read the words.

Say the sound. Trace the letters. Write the letters.

Say the words. When can you hear the /f/ sound?

Draw something beginning with **f**.

o c k -ck e u r h b f

Practise your reading and writing

Spell and write words with the focus grapheme.

1. A fat cat is in the fog.

2. A fat frog pops in the pond.

Blend to read the words and sentences.

Draw and label a picture to match one of the sentences.

Practise the sound

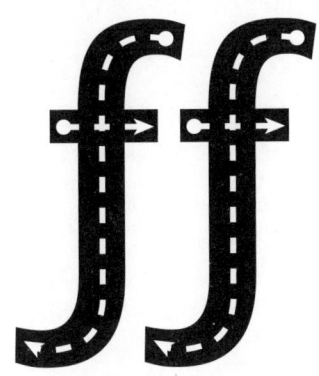

Say the sound. Trace the letters.

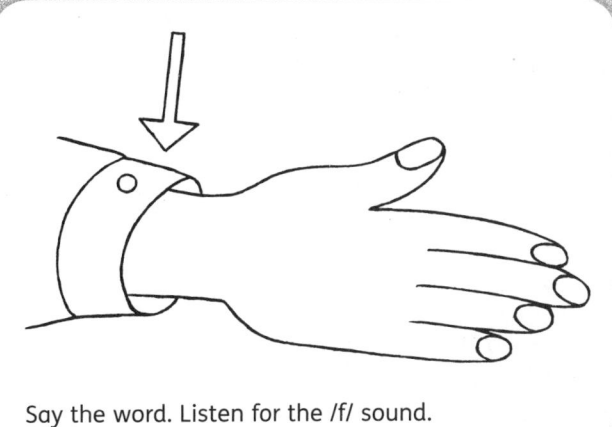

Say the word. Listen for the /f/ sound.

off huff puff cuff sniff
stuff scuff gruff puffin

Sound out and blend to read the words.

ff ff ff ff

Say the sound. Trace the letters. Write the letters.

Say the words. When can you hear the /f/ sound?

Draw something ending in **ff**.

c k -ck e u r h b f -ff

Practise your reading and writing

Spell and write words with the focus grapheme.

1. Biff huffs and puffs.

2. I pick up the stuff. The man is gruff.

Blend to read the words and sentences.

Draw and label a picture to match one of the sentences.

© Oxford University Press © Phonics International Ltd. 2020

Practise the sound

Say the sound. Trace the letter.

Say the word. Listen for the /l/ sound.

led lag let lock leg

lick slips lips list a lot

luck club slug cluck

Sound out and blend to read the words.

 l l l

Say the sound. Trace the letters. Write the letters.

Say the words. When can you hear the /l/ sound?

Draw something beginning with l.

 k -ck e u r h b f -ff l

Practise your reading and writing

Spell and write words with the focus grapheme.

1. The cat licks the milk.

2. Flick, flip, flop! The plump frogs flop into the pond.

Blend to read the words and sentences.

Draw and label a picture to match one of the sentences.

Practise the sound

Say the sound. Trace the letters.

Say the word. Listen for the /l/ sound.

ill tell mill doll fill sell

full bell gull hull hills

drill skill lollipop frills

Sound out and blend to read the words.

ll ll ll ll

Say the sound. Trace the letters. Write the letters.

Say the words. When can you hear the /l/ sound?

Draw something ending in **ll**.

-ck e u r h b f -ff l -ll

Practise your reading and writing

Spell and write words with the focus grapheme.

1. Tom and Bell go up the hill.

2. I sit still and the frogs plop into

the millpond.

Blend to read the words and sentences.

Draw and label a picture to match one of the sentences.

Practise the sound

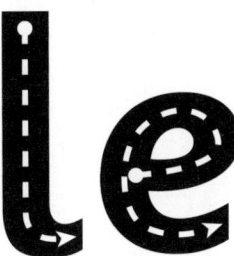

Say the sound. Trace the letters.

Say the word. Listen for the /ul/ sound.

little   kettle   middle

tickle   rattle   puddle

tackle   muddle   trickle

Sound out and blend to read the words.

le   le   le   le

Say the sound. Trace the letters. Write the letters.

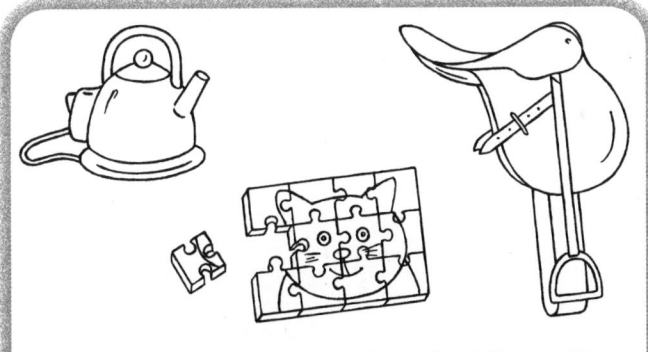

Say the words. When can you hear the /ul/ sound?

Draw something ending in **le**.

e u r h b f -ff l -ll -le

34

Practise your reading and writing

Spell and write words with the focus grapheme.

1. In the middle of the bottle is a little bug.

2. Nibble nibble, tickle tickle – the insects nip and nibble.

Blend to read the words and sentences.

Draw and label a picture to match one of the sentences.

Practise the sound

Say the sound. Trace the letters.

Say the word. Listen for the /s/ sound.

mess boss miss less

hiss toss kiss moss

fuss press cress gloss

Sound out and blend to read the words.

ss ss ss ss

Say the sound. Trace the letters. Write the letters.

Say the words. When can you hear the /s/ sound?

Draw something ending in **ss**.

u r h b f -ff l -ll -le -ss

Practise your reading and writing

Spell and write words with the focus grapheme.

1. Tess got a big kiss.

2. Miss Mac, the dress is in a mess!

Blend to read the words and sentences.

Draw and label a picture to match one of the sentences.

Say the sounds

e	f	u	m
o	c	-ss	b
-le	k	d	n
-ll	a	h	l
r	-ff	p	g
s	-ck	t	i

Oxford Reading Tree

Floppy's Phonics

Oxford Level 1+

Activity Book 1

Say the sounds and practise your reading,
spelling and handwriting skills.

Text © Oxford University Press
© Phonics International Ltd 2020

Illustrations by Oxford Designers and Illustrators

Cover Illustration by Alex Brychta

The characters in this work are the original creation
of Roderick Hunt and Alex Brychta who retain copyright
in the characters.

First published 2011
This edition published 2020

ISBN 978-1-38-200556-2

10 9
Printed in China

Paper used in the production of this book is a natural,
recyclable product made from wood grown in sustainable
forests. The manufacturing process conforms to the
environmental regulations of the country of origin.

Helping your child's learning
with free eBooks, essential
tips and fun activities
www.oxfordowl.co.uk

OXFORD
UNIVERSITY PRESS

How to get in touch:
web   www.oxfordprimary.co.uk
email primary.enquiries@oup.com
tel.   +44 (0) 1536 452610
fax   +44 (0) 1865 313472

₹ 195

ISBN 978-1-38-200556-2

9 781382 005562